Praise for Ruth Clare's memoir, *ENEMY*

"**Extraordinary memoir.**" Booktopia

"**Powerful. Stories such as Clare's must be read.**"
Books + Publishing

"**Riveting narrative.**" Australian Book Review

"**Brilliantly moving.**" Annabel Crabb, author and commentator

"**Thoroughly engaging.**" The Australian

"**A beautiful memoir about how our childhood shapes us and
the scars it leaves.**" Amra Pajalic, author

"**Heart-rending memoir, told with grace and empathy.**"
Kate Forsyth, author

"**Ruth Clare brings history into the home with piercing
intelligence, unflinching honesty and total terrifying recall.**"
Clare Wright, author of the Stella Prize-winning *The Forgotten
Rebels of Eureka*

"**An emotionally charged, powerful indictment of war and its
impact – on the lives of those who fight, and on those around
them when they return.**"
Judge's comments, Asher Literary Award

Ruth Clare is an award-winning author, TEDx speaker and educator on psychological safety, trauma recovery and resilience. She distils research informed by her science background alongside hard-won personal insights learned while overcoming a difficult childhood and living with c-PTSD and ADHD, into creative, practical strategies that allow people to step into their power and show up for their dreams.

Connect with Ruth on the socials
@ruthclareauthor

Find out more at **ruthclare.com**

*For those
quaking with doubt
but showing up anyway.*

Life Lab Books, 2025

Text copyright © Ruth Clare 2025
ruthclare.com

Cover and text design by Matt Clare
monodesign.com.au

Life
Lab
books

turn fear
into
courage

RUTH CLARE

Life
Lab
books

Fortune
favours the bold

—

ancient proverb

The power of courage

The blonde-haired producer who had greeted me in the foyer, adjusted the position of the microphone. "Stay about this far away from it, okay?" She smiled reassuringly. "You're live in thirty seconds."

My heart sprinted in response. Lucky heart. I wished I could run away too.

I had spent years hiding in a room in my house, spilling buried family secrets in a memoir, cajoling myself through the process with the promise no one ever had to read what I wrote. After Penguin bought the rights, I kept up the fantasy, that my book would somehow remain between my editor and me.

But this was live radio. A show with hundreds of thousands of listeners. I was expected to speak. Have a voice. Own my perspective. There was no turning back. My truth would be told.

It was what I thought I wanted. Validation my story was worth hearing. To help others like me know they didn't suffer alone. But looking down the barrel of the large black microphone, my joy at being chosen was swamped by the terror of being seen.

You'll say something stupid.
You'll go blank.
You'll stumble.
You aren't worth listening to.
You'll be found out as the fraud you are.

As the seconds counted down, the air felt dense with words spoken by those who had sat in the chair before me. People who were meant to be here. People who weren't me.

The host's deep, familiar voice cut across my thinking. "So, Ruth, what made you decide to write this story?"

My voice shook as I answered, but my words eventually found a rhythm. I spoke about the war my dad brought home with him that became the trauma of my childhood, and the fear that had been with me since I was a child.

After the interview, I walked along the banks of the sparkling river near the recording studio. Golden sunshine melted bones already weakened with relief now it was over. A friend who had heard the interview phoned. "You're lucky you're so confident. I could never do something like that..."

Her words struck me with their wrongness. I had been terrified and uncertain. I had no faith that it would all turn out. I was sure it would go wrong.

I wanted her to know my actions came not from confidence. Their source was much more powerful. A lifetime of learning how to build courage from fear.

Because fear was always with me. It was my most abundant emotional resource. I had learned how to transform it from lead into gold.

This book shows you how to recognise fear's disguises and tactics, how to not let it silence you, how to not let it hold you back.

This book is about courage. Owning what you have. Growing more.

I guess this book is also about confidence. The kind you earn after courage. The reward each person reaps after they have first dared to take a risk.

This book asks a question. Not, what would you do if you weren't afraid? But...

**What could you do,
who would you become,
if you learned not to let your fear stop you?**

When fear rules your life

When fear rules your life you feel stuck.
Between a rock and hard place. Between what
might be and what could happen. A lot of your
sentences start with *I can't*.

You want to unstick. But you are scared. To
rock the boat. To shake the tree. To make things
worse. To believe in yourself. To take a risk. To
fail.

You know you are unhappy with your job/
relationships/ house / career / health, and you
are utterly fed up with the sound of your own
complaining, but you can't seem to do anything
except wish things were different. You sit inert
in your stuckness, trapped in a place you don't
want to be by the prison of your own fear.

You find ways to distract yourself from
your misery – booze, food, the internet – and
for a while you spin in giddy circles that make
you forget. But fear always returns you to the

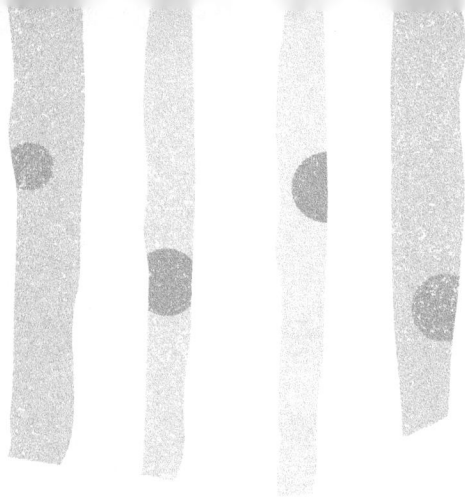

stagnant place, the place you don't want to be and the feeling of being stuck.

The stuck place where fear traps us is different for everyone. It may be a toxic relationship, an unhealthy habit, a tendency toward perfectionism, procrastination or over-concern about what other people think.

Each day you remain stuck in the prison made by fear, your feeling of powerlessness and despair grows. You worry life is passing you by and your dreams will never happen.

There is a way out. A key that will unlock your power and transform your life. That key is courage.

Why courage matters

In the crucible turning points of life, your fate is largely determined by the courage of your decisions. Courage is the catalyst that transforms the life you have into the life you want.

Courage turns who you are into who you want to be. It is an essential ingredient in all meaningful change and growth. It lets you be true to yourself, keep going beyond setbacks, live your life *on* purpose and *with* purpose. It gives you ownership of your circumstances, no matter the hand you have been dealt, so you have more choices and more power to make changes in your life.

Courage is a quality we all possess, even those of us riddled with insecurity and anxiety. Your capacity for courage is not diminished by the level of your fear. In fact, courage uses fear as fuel, so the more fear you have, the more courage you can grow.

To use our fear as courage's fuel, we must understand fear's purpose. Dare to stare deep into its eyes, without looking away. Facing fear is hard, fear being so scary and all. But if you don't want fear to stop you, it is what must be done.

Life is full of regrets. The nature of those regrets is largely determined by whether you let courage or fear define your life.

Ultimately, the decision is yours: risk regretting what you did, or what you didn't do.

Why this book

You know on some level you have outgrown the tiny corner of the ocean in which you currently swim. You want to be more and have more and create more and share more of yourself with the world. But you are crapping your pants because the ocean is full of scary fish who want to kill you.

So, you have been hiding. In your family, with your friends, at work and in the world at large. Hoping people won't see your magnificent self, secretly wishing they would.

You have spent years turning down your volume and whittling down your dreams. You never intended to live this way for so long. Somehow it has become a habit. One you aren't sure you have what it takes to break.

A part of you has been waiting, for permission, or a sign, that it is time.

That you are allowed. That it is safe. To be more. To have more. To change.

This is it. Right now. These words. This book. This is the sign you have been looking for.

Change
the rules

There is something you need to
know up front. The rules that
have governed your life so far,
aren't set in stone. You are
allowed to change them.

Want a reminder
of these rules?
Download this
as a poster at
**ruthclare.com/
resources**

THE NEW RULES
It is okay to:

1. take up space
2. have needs
3. want more
4. want less
5. want something different than you used to
6. stop doing things that don't work any more
7. say no
8. say yes
9. try new things
10. make mistakes
11. learn
12. grow
13. change your mind
14. express yourself
15. have different ideas, thoughts and perspectives than others
16. create things
17. go after what you want
18. not ask for permission
19. not get along with everyone
20. dream big
21. dream small
22. wish things were easier
23. be hopeful
24. believe in yourself
25. feel uncertain
26. take a different path
27. be who you are
28. feel whatever you feel
29. treat yourself with kindness
30. dive straight in
31. take your time
32. do nothing
33. do lots of things at once
34. not know
35. be wrong
36. show up for yourself
37. rest
38. do things that make you feel happy

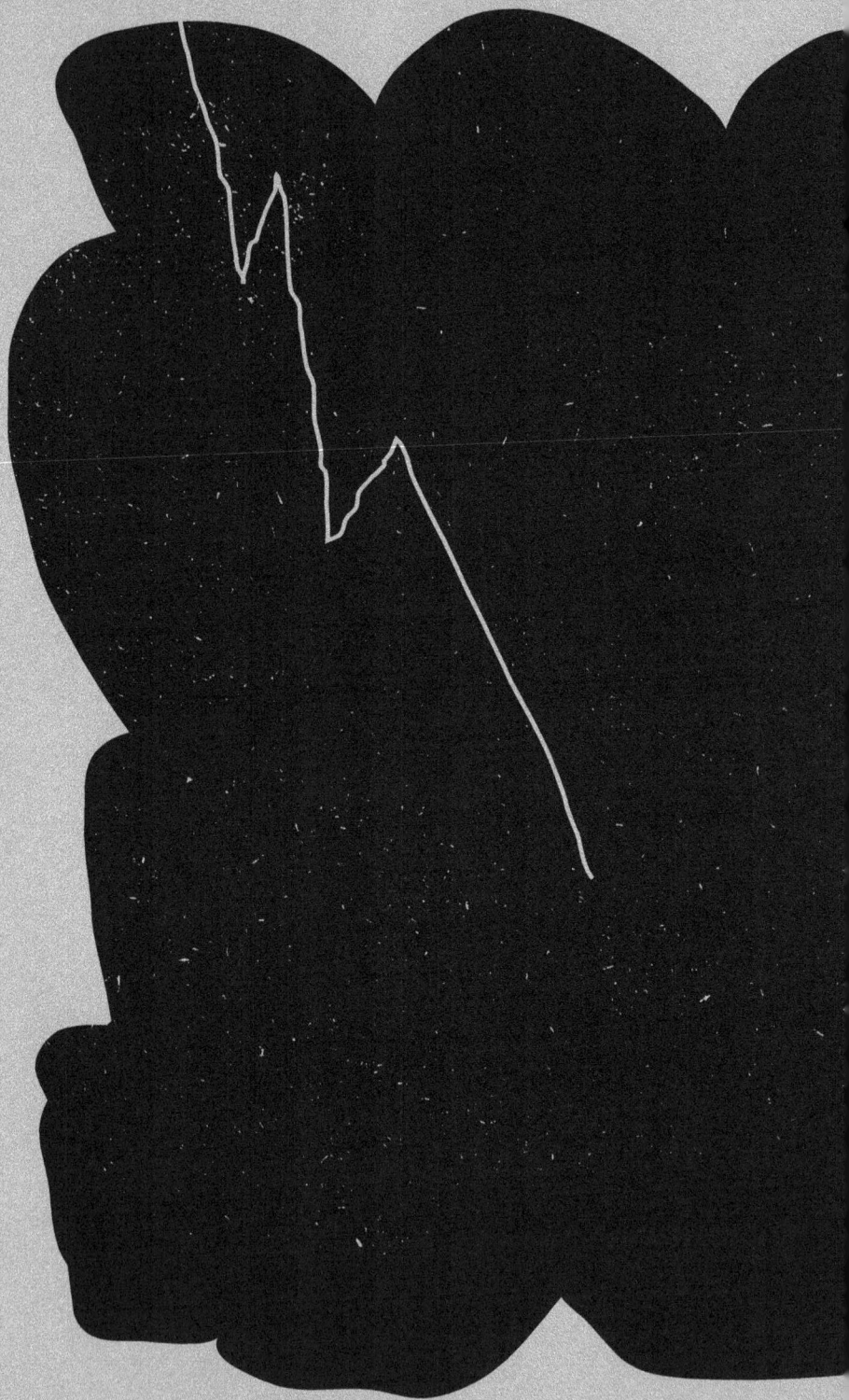

PART 1

Know your fear

*Nothing makes the light,
the wonder, the treasure
stand out so well
as darkness.*

—

Clarissa Pinkola Estés

Fear is physiological

Fear arises from the primordial ooze of our biology. It is our most ancient and primal instinct, a deep and abiding connection to our forgotten animal selves.

It may feel bizarre to think of yourself as an animal, given the way you spend your time, lost in the abstraction of technology and the interiority of your mind. But on a biological level, animal, is the foundation of who you are.

Your fear may feel distinctive, particular and personal, but its method of operation is something each mammal shares. Fear lives in all of us. It is key to the success of our species, part of our operating system, wired into our DNA.

The biology of fear

Fear begins as an impulse in a small almond-shaped mass of cells inside your brain, the amygdala, the smoke detector, the one who is always watching, keeping you safe from threats.

Fear is always felt first in the body — dragging limbs, dry mouth, hammering heart.

That is because this thing you call fear is really fight, flight, freeze, fawn, a survival response that exists in mammals everywhere.

It's your nervous system trying to help you, changing your physiology. Blood to limbs so you run faster. Shallow breaths to release the oxygen that will fuel your escape. These body responses are essential if you are squaring up against a predator. Not so effective when facing an audience on jelly legs, struggling to catch your breath.

Fear is meant to serve a functional purpose, its energy used in action, so you can get away from danger and live to tell the tale.

The sensations of fear can feel overwhelming. They can feel like an assault. But fear isn't out to get you. This ancient instinct is attempting to race you far away from danger, so you might stay safe and survive.

Fear is
a sentinel

As a child, my world was unsafe and unpredictable.

Violent father.
Alcoholic mother.
Never enough money,
to scrape by,
to go around.

Though I sometimes shook with the force of it, if you asked me if I was *afraid* growing up, I would have denied it. I hated fear. Saw the way it held my mother in its grip, making her a target, leaving her incapacitated and exposed.

I hid my fear behind a show of confidence, striving and achievement, lest anyone ever see just how vulnerable and afraid I truly was.

I didn't know that no matter how I scorned and rejected my fear, it would always stand sentinel beside me, doing its best to keep me safe so I could live to fight another day. So much energy I wasted, trying to pretend my fear wasn't there, instead of harnessing the energy it offered like a gift.

Fear is not the enemy

Fear is the potent force that stands in the way of where you are and where you want to be. It drives your procrastination and self-doubt, your people pleasing and perfectionism. Living beneath its thumb shrinks your spirit, stunts your growth and turns you into a shadow of the person you were born to be.

Knowing this, it makes sense that you might wish to get rid of your fear. With fear out of the way, surely then you would be free to do more and be more and have more of the life you want? Removal of your fear is not only unnecessary, it is impossible.

Fear is an indelible part of who you are. It is a primal instinct that exists only for your benefit. It has one goal and one goal only: to keep you alive. Without it, you would stray into traffic, jump off cliffs and haplessly wander into packs of marauding wolves. Fear is essential to your survival. It is a companion until death do you part. But it is not designed to be in the driving seat of your life.

Instead of wasting energy attempting to get rid of your fear, the trick is learning to own it, accept it and channel its energy into courage.

How fear
holds you back

To stop being ruled by your fear, you must understand what fear is and fear isn't. That begins by recognising that fear is not interested in self-mastery, self-discovery or self-actualisation. The predominant impulse that drives fear is self-preservation.

Better the devil you know is fear's modus operandi. Even if the devil makes you miserable every day.

Fear is a risk analyst on steroids. It sees danger everywhere and is only happy when you are wrapped in cotton wool. If fear had its way you would live in a cave, dark and isolated, hidden and safe.

The downside to this, is that outside of the cave, in the uncomfortable and unfamiliar brightness, is where the joyful adventure of life happens. Uncomfortable and unfamiliar are where the life you want awaits.

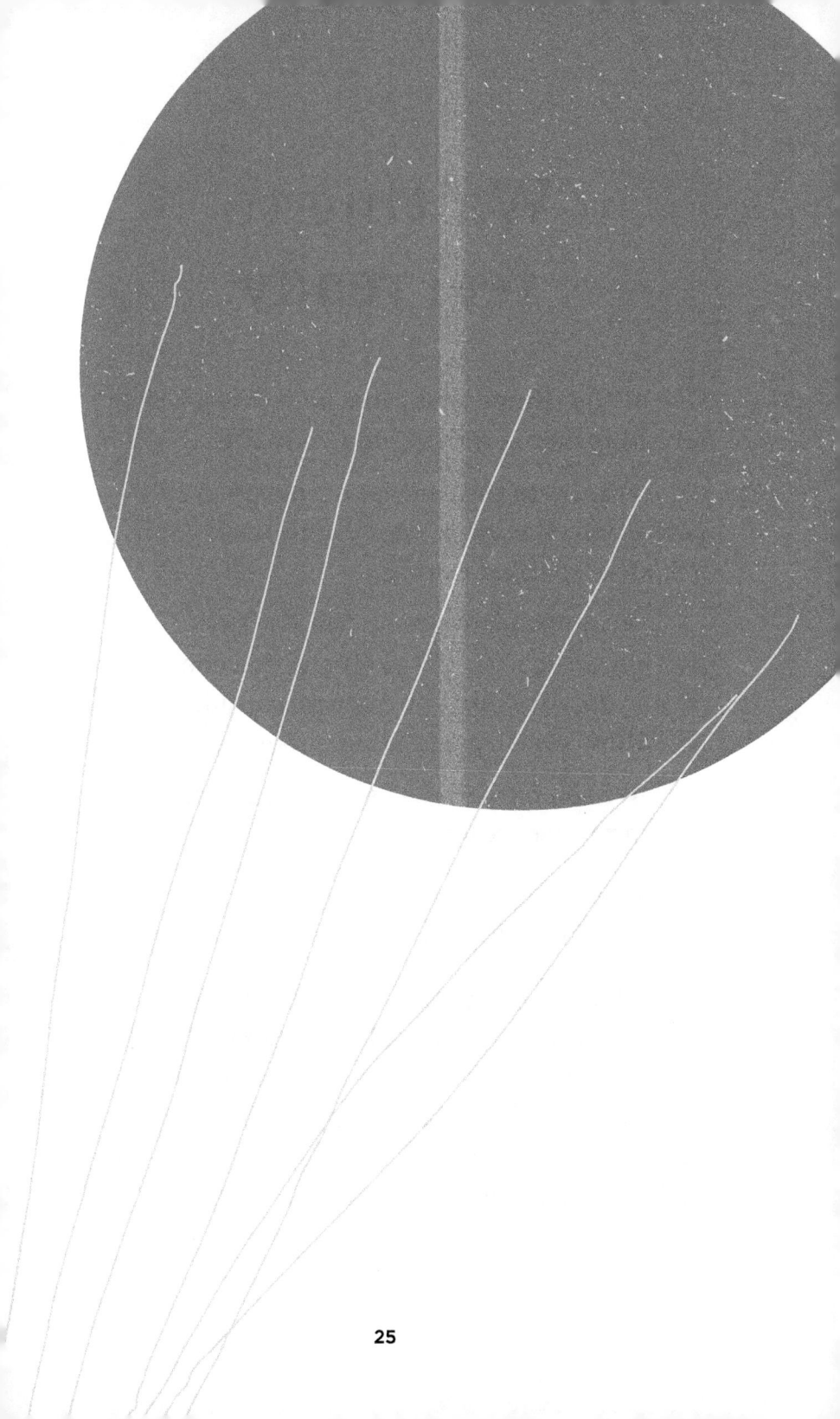

Waiting to feel ready

One of the things that kills more dreams than anything else is waiting to feel ready.

Fear loves the concept of imagined perfection. *Complete knowledge, ideal decisions, perfect timing.*

Fear spends years on the fantasy of getting things "right", as if there is one correct way to do something or a secret method that will allow you to avoid all mistakes.

We tell ourselves that we are simply waiting to feel ready.

Know this.
You may never feel ready.

There is not a single life-altering choice I have made that I felt ready for. Admitting I was struggling and needed help, setting my first boundary, publicly sharing my story. Every time I felt like a child wobbling chaotically, terrified of falling, as they learned to ride a bike.

If you are challenging yourself to grow, trying new approaches, breaking old patterns of behaviour, learning new ways of thinking, daring to step into unchartered territory, you may always feel afraid.

Tolerating fear is an essential skill for all growth and change.

Feeling ready is not required.

Science concepts to understand

POTENTIAL ENERGY

Potential energy is the energy stored in an object due to its position, its properties and the forces acting upon it. Picture the effort it takes to draw an arrow in a bow.

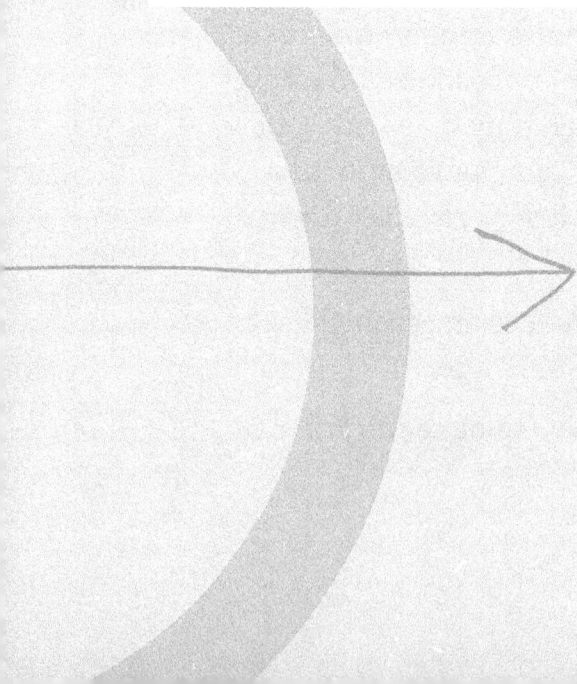

KINETIC ENERGY

Kinetic energy is the energy of motion.
The release of energy that happens
when the arrow is fired.

The first law of thermodynamics states that
energy is neither created nor destroyed, only
transformed into different states.

**Just as potential energy can be
transformed into kinetic energy,
fear can be transformed into courage**

**The process is the same.
You have to let the arrow fly.**

Unleashing the powerful potential of fear

Fear locks you in the moment of potential, trapping you in a state of non-doing.

Fear takes all the energy you have spent pulling your arrow back in the bow (*I want this. I want to change that.*) and holds you there, bombarding you, exhausting you, with nightmares of what might be, what could happen, if you let your arrow fly.

Fear wants to believe there is a way you can let your arrow go, have it fire along the ideal, straight-line trajectory and land with a satisfying thud. Bullseye every time.

But real life isn't like that. So, fear convinces you it is safer to stay frozen. Take no risks. Make no moves, lest they turn out to be wrong. Fear is not meant to trap us in this way.

Though our days may no longer be spent hunting and gathering, fear's purpose and function remains the same. Fear is fuel to drive action.

To turn fear into courage,
you must transform
potential to kinetic energy.
Move from thinking to doing.

Break free from the fantasy
of imagined perfection.
**Embrace the messy reality
of good enough**

Only through action
does your energy activate.
Only through action
do dreams become reality.

**Only through action
can you use fear's power
for good.**

Fear sees in black and white

Fear is connected to the less evolved part of our brain. It is not known for its nuance of thought. Like a conspiracy theorist, locked in its bedroom, it clutches at straws, turning random events into Ultimate Truths. It sits in its bias, spins like a doctor and tells you it knows Who You Are, What People Are Like and How The World Is.

Fear puts cause and effect together in a haphazard fashion, following no rhyme or reason, but always believing it is right.

He is angry, it must be my fault.

If I admit I was wrong, she will leave me.

I was not chosen, it is all a conspiracy, life is out to get me, I am always despised.

Fear sees in black and white.
It believes in hard and fast rules.

Right | Wrong
Good | Bad
All | Nothing
Us | Them

Fear swings wildly between extremes.

Nothing your fault | Everything your fault
I am the worst | You are the worst

It speaks in absolutes.

Everything
Always
Nothing
Never

When these words occupy your thoughts or
language, be on alert, for it is fear doing
the talking.

Become aware of the generalisations you have made, built on the limited perspective of your fear.

You fail one exam;
you are stupid.

One person hurts you;
all people will hurt you.

She wins the prize;
it will never be you.

Fear is trying to prevent you from doing things that might lead you to be hurt. But its method of achieving this goal is a little on the nose.

Examine the limiting ideas you have about what you are capable of and the choices available to you.

Come to recognise them for what they are: ill conceived ideas based on fear's limited capacity for complex thought.

Fear is
a storyteller

Fear will tell you anything to help you stay safe.

It will criticise, belittle and sabotage. It will tell you it knows the future.

Fear will lie and double cross you, give you enough rope to hang yourself, then hog-tie you and throw you to the ground... *for your own good.*

Fear has no scruples. It doesn't care what it has to do. Fear has been tangled so long in its own web of bullshit it no longer even knows it is lying. But make no mistake, Fear is a liar.

It will bewitch you with long and elaborate stories. Beware these stories. Come to know them and to see them for what they are: myths made of fear.

THE FEAR STORIES

The PAST DEFINES FUTURE story

If you failed in the past, you will fail in the future. If you were hurt in the past, you will only experience more hurt. If you challenge the stories of your family or your history, dare to walk a different path or move in a new direction, bad things will happen. If you step outside of the role assigned to you, challenge people on their crap behaviour, reach for more, try things you haven't done before, tragedy will befall you. Your past is the person you are and you don't get a choice about the person you become. You must get what you get and not get upset. You don't have a say in your destiny, and all your efforts to change the way things currently are will be so disastrous that you will lose everything you currently have, end up living on the street, where you will be attacked by a horde of marauding strangers, potentially even zombies, and you will die.

FEAR STORY 2:
The YOU WILL NEVER RECOVER story

If you shake things up, speak your truth, go after what you want, dare to live more joyfully, you will blow your world apart. Change and growth is a point of no return. All the choices you make are permanent. They can't be rewound or undone. Taking new steps in a different, more life-affirming direction will produce irreversible and life-altering consequences. The consequences for taking this action may include being kicked out of your house and abandoned on the street... where the zombies are waiting to kill you. This death will be horrifying. Seriously. Disembowelling, the whole nine yards. Don't start. It's not worth it. Who needs that?

The YOU WILL BECOME POOR story

If you take a risk of any sort you will lose all of your money. Your house... gone. Your savings... gone. You will be forced to live on the street. Did I mention there are zombies out there? And because you didn't play it safe, we now don't have a house. So, thanks for that. Thanks a lot.

The YOU WILL LOOK STUPID story

If you ask questions, wear something different, share your thoughts, go for the promotion, try selling something on Etsy, or do anything that in any way makes you stand out instead of fitting in, people will think you are a moron, laugh at you and talk about you behind your back. When you fail miserably, which you inevitably will, and you come grovelling back to your old life with your tail between your legs, the stink of your stupidity will be so strong people will not want to come within 500 metres of you. You will become unemployable. No job = no money = no house. Why not just offer us up to the zombies right now? Seriously.

The YOU WILL BE HATED BY THOSE YOU LOVE story

If, in pursuit of authentic identity or truth, happiness or peace, passion or purpose, you irritate, challenge, inconvenience or in any way disappoint others, you will be despised. If you don't say the exact words people want to hear at all times, find the perfect time to slot your dreams in around everyone else's needs, and have an iron-clad guarantee of success for everything you attempt, everyone – your partner, your children, your parents, your friends, that weird cousin you only met once and who smelled like fish – will think you are a horrible, selfish and unlovable human being. It's not just the people who know you directly, either. All the people in your neighbourhood, your society, your race, your community, they will all hate you too.

Because you are so despised, you will be kicked out of the house and forced to live under a bridge, where the zombies will find you. And as you run from these zombies in terror, desperately banging on people's front doors pleading for help, they will stand in the safety of their homes shaking their heads at your plight. They will say *this is only what you deserve.* They will turn their backs on you as the zombies close in, and soon you too will be wandering the streets drooling with an insatiable hunger for human flesh.

The stories fear is telling you may be trying to help you avoid risk, but it opens you up to another risk: that life passes you by without you ever truly living. Statistically speaking, that is a much greater risk than being attacked by zombies. For now, at least...

There is no avoiding trouble

Fear acts like it can predict the future. It tells you it *knows* what will happen. This is a delusion aimed at creating certainty where none exists.

Helen Keller said, "Avoiding danger is no safer in the long run than outright exposure. The fearful are caught as often as the bold."

What fear doesn't want you to know is that ready or not, the world is coming. Ready or not, change will happen. Trying to keep things the way they are, doesn't stop the unexpected or unwanted from transpiring.

People die. Jobs are made redundant. Accidents happen.

You can do your best to steer away from misfortune and missteps, to win friends and influence people, but much as you might wish otherwise, you don't get to choose many of the events that happen in your life.

Fear tells us the way to navigate this is to stay small and not stick our heads out of our caves in case they are bitten off. This instinct made sense when sabre tooth tigers were lurking. It serves us less well in the modern world, leading us to shrink from opportunities to change, grow and lead.

The way to stop living through the perspective of your fear is through pragmatic acceptance of the messiness of life. You will try new things of your own choosing – behaviours, relationships, careers. Sometimes these things will go great. Sometimes they won't turn out as you hoped. There are times you will come up short, probably more than you would like.

You will face challenges you didn't choose. They will often feel painful, unfair, chaotic and really, really hard. If you don't give up, you will mostly figure out a way to respond. This may take longer than you expect and lead you in directions you didn't anticipate.

Sometimes you will overcome things. Sometimes you will just learn to live with them. Either way, life will go on, because that is what life does.

Life happens no matter how much you hide from it, so you may as well start living it instead. Go after what you want. Say what you mean. Celebrate moments of joy. Do what you can to create more happiness for yourself.

Life only happens once.
This is yours.

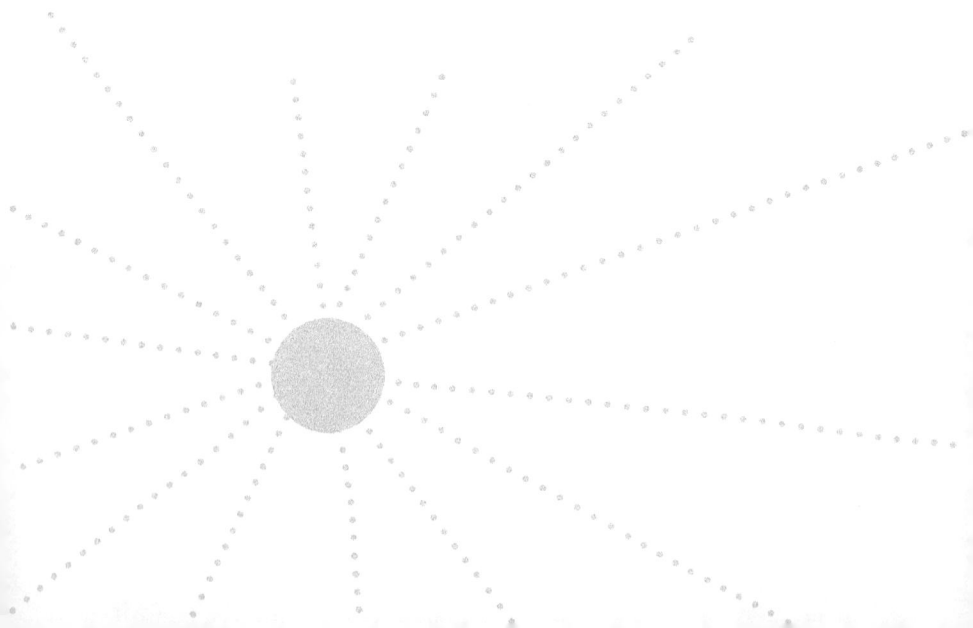

Fear
hates change

Given free rein fear would have you doing exactly the same thing you did the day before. It would stop you from growing in any way because when you grow things change.

change = uncertainty = risk

Fear can arise when you create art or businesses or families; when you make changes on the inside or the outside; when you confront the past or aim for the future.

It can appear when you own difficult truths, or dare to accept yourself, be yourself or back yourself. It can appear when you prioritise your needs, create plans for your life or dare to find a way forward, to rise up, to be happy, no matter what.

Instead of being dismayed or disheartened because fear has appeared yet again, learn to embrace it as a sign of your growth. Fear is an essential element in all true transformation. Its energy gives you the power you need to shake yourself out of the familiar, so you can evolve into the version of yourself you always wished to be.

Fear is part of the process of stretching and expanding. It appears each time you risk or reveal yourself. The higher you reach, the more honestly you show yourself to others, the stronger the fear you feel.

Instead of seeing fear as a sign something is going wrong, open yourself up to the possibility that it might mean something is going right.

Be your own fairy godmother

When I was young I spent a lot of time playing Cinderella, waiting and wishing for a fairy godmother to wave a wand over my ugly life and turn me into a beautiful princess. In adulthood, this idea stood me outside of my power, waiting for something or someone else to change so my life could be transformed.

Fear is our guardian; but it perennially sees us as the children we once were. It convinces us that magical thinking is a solution, and our job is to wait for the grownups to save us.

Growing bigger than your fear begins with recognising you are grown.

There is grief in this. It means no one is coming. It means owning that you are the adult. That the choices you are making, the actions you are taking, the life you are creating, isn't up to anyone but you.

This may seem destabilizing. So much responsibility you must bear. It is also cause for celebration. You are an adult! Free to decide. Able to make changes. To write your own rules. Make your own plans. Decide how you are going to live.

Fear has helped you to survive until now. It will always be there to protect you. But it has taken you as far as it can. Fear is not equipped to lead you where you want to go.

It is time to become the hero of your story. It's time to grow bigger than your fear.

PART 2

Grow bigger than your fear

The braver I am,
the luckier I get.

—

Glennon Doyle

Overcoming the fawn response

I learnt to fawn from the very start. Keep my opinions to myself lest they trigger my father's rage. Keep my needs to myself in case they made my mum drink more. My fawning came from fear that I was an unlovable, unworthy burden destined to be cast out from the tribe, for things I didn't understand, just for being me.

I survived through pleasing and appeasing, became a chameleon, an actor, second-guessing every word, performing for everyone all the time, the world was my stage. The only way I felt safe was to hide behind a mask, to never be myself with anyone, to put on an exhausting, constant show of what others wanted me to be.

When my mum was too drunk to pick me up from basketball practice or watch me in the school play, I said, "I don't mind. Don't worry about it. Of course I understand."

"I know I don't have to worry with you," she would reply. "You've always been such an easy kid."

Her words were a badge of honour.

Good girl.
Nice girl.
No trouble at all.

All I had to do for these scraps of approval, was say yes when my heart screamed no, place everyone's needs above my own and bend over backwards until my back gave way. All I had to do was endlessly scan people's emotions, predict the needs of others and ensure I made them more important than my own.

All I had to do was abandon myself over and over, ignoring my feelings, my instincts, my thoughts, whatever it took, whatever they wanted, so they didn't cast me aside.

As children we depend on our parents and other adults for our survival. The world we operate within is largely defined by them. In my house, speaking my mind, sharing an opinion, or existing outside of the tight parameters of my father's approval was met with swift punishment. Back then, the fear-based rules *stay hidden, stay safe, don't rock the boat* helped keep me safe.

Cheryl Strayed said, "Don't surrender all your joy for an idea you used to have about yourself that isn't true anymore."

We need to be wary about our own outdated ideas about ourselves.

Growing bigger than your fear begins by recognising that the landscape you are operating in is not the same as it once was. You no longer need to forsake yourself or relinquish your dreams, ideas and needs so as not to be a bother to others.

You don't have prove anything to anyone. Not the people from your past who hurt you, or your kids or your friends or some rando on social media.

Challenge those thoughts that made sense in the past and see if they really apply to your life today.

You get
to decide

I am sorry if anyone made you feel broken or unloveable or less than. I am sorry if you felt like you had to be perfect or different to the way you are, to win love and approval. But I want you to know that no matter how damaging people's behaviour has been, or how convincing these arguments may have seemed, or how many times you have repeated these ideas inside your own head, they aren't true. Just, no.

Your fear may have convinced you that the circumstance of your past is a roadmap for your future. Your fear may have told you it isn't safe to have hope, or to be yourself or to want anything from life. To steer you away from the disappointment of wanting things you may not get, or loving people who could hurt you, your fear may even have told you that you don't deserve the good things others have.

Fear will say anything to protect you.

Poor misguided fear. Trying to be helpful. Making it worse.

Know this: *Fear has got it wrong.*

You are lovely and loveable just as you are. Even if you don't look the way you think you should or haven't achieved as much as you thought you might or aren't as confident or rich or funny as you would like to be. You, as much as any other, deserve all the good things in life. Yes, you.

You deserve joy and love. You deserve rest and nourishment. You deserve to live a meaningful life. You deserve to spend time doing things that make you happy with people that celebrate who you are. Not because of anything you have done. Just because that's what we all deserve.

Psychologist, Dr Nicola Le Pera said, "Most of our limits exist within our thoughts. Thoughts are not truths." You don't have to keep imposing limits on what is possible for you, simply because you have fallen into the habit of doing so. Your thoughts are not truths no matter how many times you might have thought them.

You can live in a different way. You can choose to be kind and gentle with yourself and to surround yourself with people who see your worth. You are entitled to take up space and shine that dazzling light you have been hiding for so long.

You have permission to prioritise living your life in a way that honours the truth of who you are over living for the approval of others. You get to have a choice and a say in how you spend your time, what thoughts you choose to listen to and the people you allow into your heart. It is possible to take back the power you have spent your life giving away.

The ideas that served you in the past, aren't serving you now. Just because they feel familiar, doesn't mean they are true. Your life changes when you stop looking for evidence of your own unworthiness and start believing you are fine as you are.

You might feel like a phony when you first try this. All new things feel strange at the start. Believe in your own inherent loveability, even if that concept is foreign to you.

How? Think of the mammal in the world you love best. For me, it is a dog. Specifically, my golden retriever cross, Fred. Feel the tender feelings you feel toward your mammal and picture that mammal living inside you.

This is less far-fetched than it sounds, for you too are simply a mammal. With a too-big brain and a too-ancient nervous system, struggling to survive in a world more complicated than anything our ancestors could have imagined. Like my darling boy, Fred, you are loveable. Of course you are. I can see it from here.

You don't need to prove your worth to anyone.

Living from this foundational knowing, that you are worthy just as you are, allows you to turn up more authentically and persist more enthusiastically.

This sets off a chain reaction that gathers its own momentum. It is a process of radical growth that most quickly sets you free.

What if there was less wrong than you think?

Your fear's only desire is to help you survive. It is not interested in what is good and right with the world. Its priority is to identify everything that *is* wrong or *could be* wrong or *might go* wrong to help you avoid them.

From an evolutionary perspective this makes sense. The people who knew where the sabre tooth tiger hid or which bush contained poisonous berries were the ones that survived long enough to reproduce. But the tendency of our brain to notice only what is wrong with life is a real drag. It can keep us miserable even at times of peace and plenty. It can rob us of the capacity for joy and rest.

You must come to recognise the negativity bias in your wiring. Only then can you balance fear's constant hungry search for all that is wrong, with appreciation and gratitude for everything that's wonderful, joyful and right.

Test your own negativity bias now

- Name five things you **don't like** about yourself.

- Name five things you **love** about who you are.

- Name five life **problems** you are currently facing.

- Name five things you have **accomplished** this year.

- Name five **hurtful** things people have said to you.

- Name five **lovely** things people have told you about yourself.

Which of these tasks were easier?

Amplify
the positive

Without awareness of our biological bias toward negativity we can come to believe the worries and problems we spend most of our energy focusing on are the only things that exist. We can fail to notice the positive, joyful, light moments that fill our days too.

It takes some effort to work against an innate tendency of our physiology, but it is possible.

FIGHT YOUR NEGATIVITY BIAS

If someone gives you a compliment, take a moment to breathe it in.

If you achieve a task, pause long enough to celebrate your own kick-arsery.

Spend time each day savouring changing seasons and growing gardens and loving animals and delicious food and kind people and the pleasure of sliding each night into the soft warmth of your bed.

Good things happen each day.
Noticing these positive moments allows you
to relax. It reminds you that you that you
have much to celebrate and feel grateful for.

**The more gratitude you have,
the less fear you feel.**

Come back to the present

Instead of using fear's energy the way it is intended to be used – to drive action – many of us channel it into overthinking. We convince ourselves worrying is a form of planning, as if preparing for worst case scenarios will stop them happening, and re-hashing past events will alter them.

The problem with this is that your highly evolved brain is not great at distinguishing the images you are creating in your mind from reality. It sees the painful memories and terrible futures you are picturing and thinks they are real. Your body responds as if it is facing the threat in real time, activating your fight, flight, freeze, fawn response. Your muscles clench, your heart speeds, you feel stressed and overwhelmed.

**Your endless thinking
is not a safety net.
It is a trap.
The person you have caught
is yourself.**

To escape, you must first become aware of what you are doing.

PRESENT MOMENT PRACTICE:

Stop thinking and breathe. Look around you right now. Are you safe? Stop living in your head and come back to the present moment. Experience the world through your senses. What do you see, hear, smell, taste, touch? Feel your feet in your shoes. Notice the place your bottom interacts with the seat you are sitting in. Return to the physical and tangible world within and around you.

Most times your fear is unfounded. A figment of your imagination. Remind yourself of that. All you have to do is stop thinking those thoughts and return to the moment you are in.

This moment. Right now. The only one you ever have the power to change.

Stay in your own lane

Fear says...

> *you don't understand.*
> *how hard it has been.*
> *how much I have had to deal with.*
> *how easy it is for others*
> *but not for me.*

I would never want to diminish how much you have endured. It amazes me that any of us manage to stagger through life after all we have been through. You will find no argument from me that the world is deeply unfair and many people, yourself included, have experienced very real injustice and adversity.

> **Life being unfair is a fact.**
> **That fact doesn't have to stop you.**

Your fear may taunt you with people who have millions of followers and millions of dollars. It may compare you to them, making your dreams feel unsurmountable and your resources seem inadequate.

At first this might seem cruel. It's all part of fear's grand agenda. Fear is hoping to convince you to give up your efforts and shrink into the back of the cave where you are safe.

Growing bigger than your fear means learning to stay in your own lane. Instead of looking left and right – at what he is doing, what she has got – look ahead to your destination. Importantly, look behind, at how far you have already come.

Think back to the starting point of your child self. See the place you started. See the place you are now.

**Honour your own unfurling,
the worlds you have traversed,
all that you have learned,
the amazing person
you have already become.**

First, contain your fear

I have studied science and psychotherapy and counselling. I have read hundreds of books on psychology and spent years inside rooms of therapists of all persuasions. I have tried to figure out and "fix myself" in a hundred ways that involved attempting to intellectualize my pain away.

What I wished I understood while I tried to think my way out of the patterns of my past was this: until you learn to calm your frightened animal self, you can never be at peace.

Trying to think your way out of your feelings is a desperate attempt to feel more in control so you can feel safe. This overthinking is the very thing that traps you in survival mode. It is far wiser to go direct to the source, and to build a feeling of safety in your body.

FEAR CONTAINING PRACTICE 1:

BREATHE

... Fear makes your breathing shallow, readying you to take flight. Notice this. Change it.

... Follow your breath as it enters your nostrils and travel with it to the dense and quiet container of your body. Stay with it as it makes your stomach rise. Make the outbreath longer. In for three, out for four. In for four, out for five. In for five, out for six.

... Slow your breathing, slow your thinking, reduce your fear.

Detatch from THOUGHTS

... Fear thoughts are sticky. They overpower other thoughts. Learn to notice when you are caught by them and step back inside your mind.

... Become the observer. Expand to the place of witness. Watch fear thoughts without inhabiting them. Notice when they pick you up (they always pick you up). Step back. Do this over and over until they begin to pass you by.

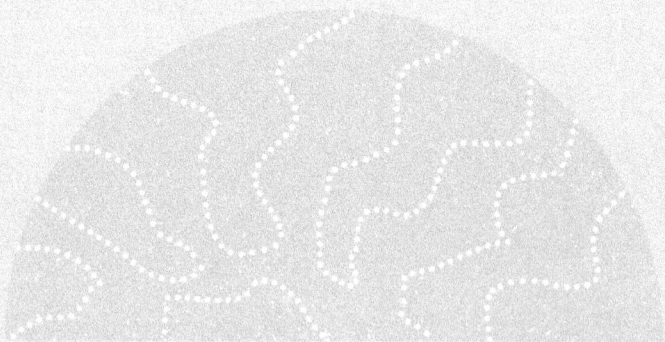

MOVE

... Fear's energy is made to prime our bodies for escape. Lean into this.

... Release the excess through activity – dancing, walking, yoga, weightlifting, running, swimming. Make the movement match the intensity until your fear levels out.

Connect with NATURE

... Step away from your screens and ground through your animal self. Return to the calm of nature – ocean, mountains, forest – and experience the world through your senses.

... Hear, see, smell, taste and touch. Come back to the peaceful present, where the sun warms your face, the birds sing their song and the pine scent of the forest fills you with a feeling of the world being right again.

Own your fears so they don't own you

To gain power over your fears, you must be willing to look them in the eye. Instead of allowing your fears to own you, grow big enough to own them instead.

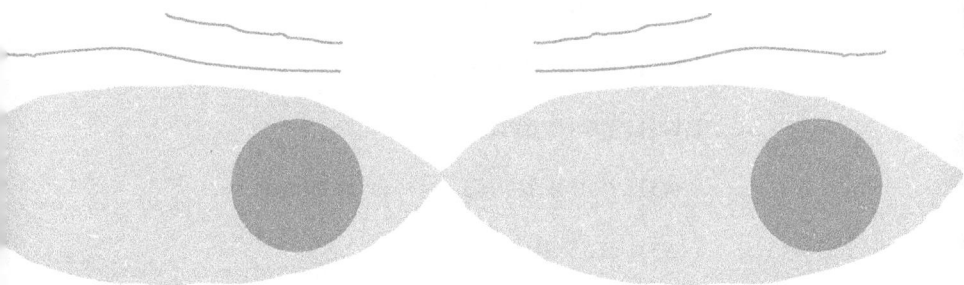

Today my fear says ...

... the look my boss gave me means I am in trouble and I will be fired

... my partner doesn't love me any more

... I am not a good mother

... my friends won't like me if they know what I am really like

... I am too ugly/ fat/ skinny/ old/ short/ tall / dumb /unsuccessful/ poor to be loved

... I will be left behind

... I will be overlooked

... I will die and no one will care

... I will not succeed

... the road is too hard and long

... life works for others but not for me

Staring your fears down separates you from them. It reminds you your fears are not all of who you are.

Once those fears are on the page, tear them from your book, scrunch them in your hand, throw them in the bin, burn them in the fire. Look in the mirror and say three times

I own my fears and let them go.
I am bigger than my fears.

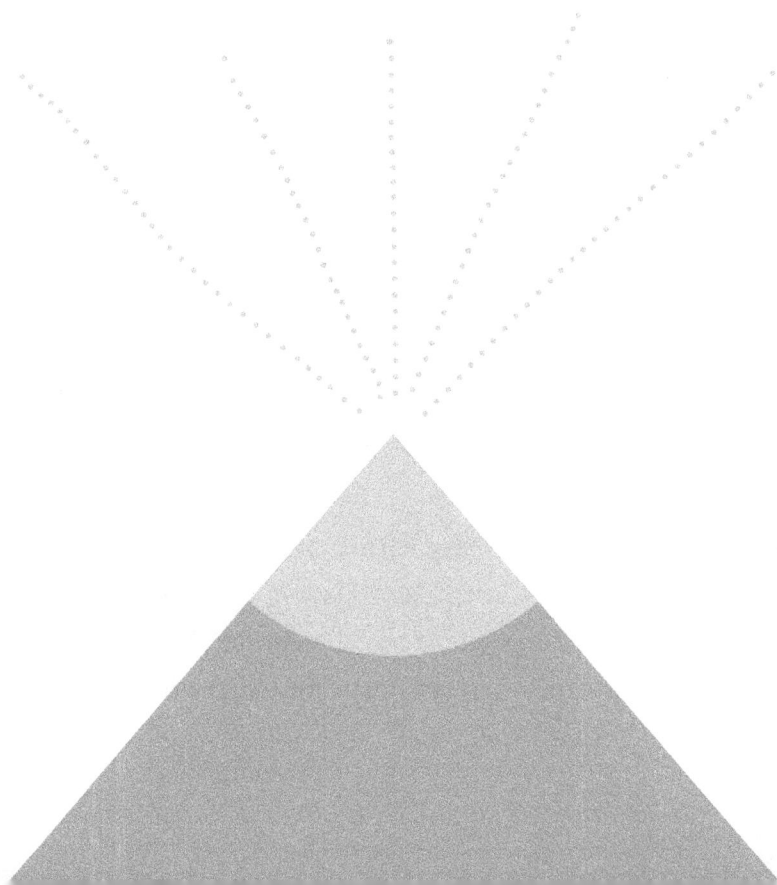

Overriding fear

I am driving an hour outside of Melbourne to an audience of 600 year twelve students. It is the biggest audience I have faced. I am the embodiment of imposter syndrome, racked with self-doubt.

The slides I spent weeks preparing contain memes to lighten a more serious discussion about mental health. What was I thinking? Trying to be funny. They are teenagers. They will not find someone their mum's age funny. They will think I am pathetic. Sad and pathetic and boring. Do year twelves even look at memes any more?

My heart hammers in my chest. The whoosh of blood in my ears is as loud as the thrumming of the tyres on the road beneath me. My throat is strangled. My breathing a pant. It is fear. Trying to rob me of my voice so I stay quiet and safe.

Fear speaks in my mind. *Why do you do this? Stand on stage? Share your stories? Speak your truth? It's dangerous. It's ludicrous. You have nothing to say, nothing anyone wants to hear.*

I imagine similar thoughts galloping through the mind of Henry Fonda, who, even at 75 used to throw up with nerves each night before a stage performance. Like him, I know that when I step on stage the fear will disappear. But I am not on stage yet.

I am in the before time, the time when fear makes its most fervent efforts, a last-ditch attempt to throw me off my game. Fear sweeps me up for a minute and I see in my mind a high definition, digital surround sound image of myself on stage. There is booing. Choruses of *You suck! Shut up you moron!* Fruits are being thrown.

Instead of following where those thoughts are leading me, I turn on the radio, switch stations until I hear a song I know. I train my full awareness to the words blasting at me through the speakers, singing along with them as loud as I can, unlocking my voice, reclaiming my breath, showing my fear that I refuse to be cowed.

Fear's radio station keeps interrupting. *Who do you think you are? You don't know anything about anything. It's going to go wrong.* I speak aloud, to the frightened animal inside me, who is believing all fear's stories and wants to run away and hide.

It is all good, little darling. You are safe. You will be great. And if you suck, no one will die, no one will get angry. You will just have done a bit of a crap job. But you never have before, so I have total faith you won't now.

I address fear directly. *Hey Fear! All the chit-chat is not helpful right now. The only way out of this thing is through it, so how about you get out of my way?*

I draw in my breath, *in for four, hold for four, out for four, hold for four.* I feel my feet in my shoes, bringing my awareness back this moment, where life is good and I am safe. When the car has stopped, I walk until I find a quiet spot and jump up and down for a minute, discharging the adrenaline fear has supplied in excess amounts.

I put my hands on my hips and spread my legs out wide for a moment and raise my hands up to the sky, giving feedback to tightened muscles that it is okay to take up space and strut my stuff on stage. I might look silly. So what? Silly is better than scared. I punch the air above me like I am a rock star, then laugh at my own ridiculousness and have a drink of water.

The crowd is loud and unruly as I enter. Teen prisoners on a day trip out of the cells of

their classrooms. I stand on stage and do my best. I take my focus off myself and connect to the audience instead. Not *what are you thinking of me* but *I really hope this helps.*

Am I Brené Brown? No. Am I Mel Robbins? No. I am myself. Try-hard funny memes and all.

After I am done, a girl approaches, tells me she had never heard someone share a story like mine, that it made her feel better, to know it is not just her. Another student tells me they found my talk helpful, they have been grappling with depression, and they are going to try some of the things I shared.

Fear tries to convinces us our pain is not okay, our stories are unacceptable, vulnerability makes us weak, that we do not belong.

It is trying to protect us. In doing so, it isolates us from the thing that can most deeply help us: to know that we all struggle, we all hurt, but that we are not alone.

Back on the highway driving home, my perfectionism, fear's minion, wants to erase all the good moments with the mistakes. I do not let it. I have faced my biggest crowd. I was not perfect, but good. I did something scary and I survived.

Growing is uncomfortable

Growing requires you to shed the old skin that is constraining you so you might step into a bigger version of the person that you are.

This process can make you feel naked. Familiar skin you knew so well no longer fitting; new skin not fully formed. It can leave you feeling vulnerable and uncertain, unprotected and afraid.

**Discomfort is part of the process.
A price that must be paid for evolution
and transformation. It is sign you are
becoming the person you always
wanted to be.**

Fear almost stopped me

When I began writing this book, my fear almost stopped me.

It told me writing about fear was asking for trouble. *Don't open up this box of worms. You're making yourself a target. You don't know what you're talking about. Get back in the cave.*

It told me no one would read it.

Fear isn't something people want to know about. No one will even read this book. What a waste of your life. Is that how you want to spend your precious time on this earth? Writing books no one wants to read?

It told me how much those who did read this book would hate it.

People will despise this book. They will laugh at you. They will judge you. They will throw it in the bin.

When I continued regardless, it started ranting like it was drunk.

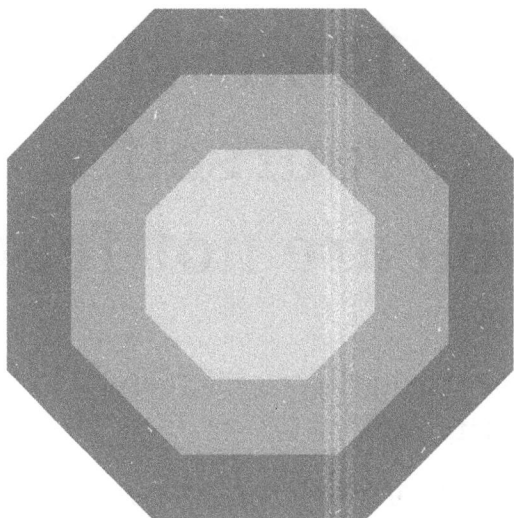

Who are you to talk about fear? You want people to think you're brave, but I know your bullshit. You are terrified. No one will listen to you. You will look like an idiot. People will get together and talk about what a gargantuan fool you are. Your friends will feel sorry for you and the rest of the world will despise you. Give up now.

Each day I heard the stories and kept putting words on the page. There is no great trick to it. No great 'fear eradication tool'.

Feel scared.
Keep going.
Repeat.

Remind yourself you are not fear

Instead of attempting to rid yourself of fear, stop identifying with it.

Not *I am afraid* but *I am experiencing fear.*

This inch of separation allows you to see it, name it, and loosen the stranglehold that entangles you in its grasp. *I am experiencing* not *I am* is a reminder of the truth:

You are not your feelings
You are the one who feels

Harden yourself to the fool

In French there is a phrase about courage. –

*Le courage est à mi-chemin entre
la lâcheté et la témérité.*

Loosely translated, it means courage is the median between cowardice and foolhardiness. What strikes me most about this saying is the word foolhardy.

I know this is not the correct definition, foolhardy meaning reckless, but I like the idea of foolhardy meaning "hardening yourself to looking like a fool". Not taking yourself too seriously is a powerful way to grow your courage.

The hard fact of it is, sometimes when you are being bold and courageous, you are going to put your arrow in the bow, draw it back, let it fly, and the damn thing is going to slip from your fingers and drop at your feet.

You are going to launch a product that doesn't work or put on a lame party or end up in a relationship with some bozo who ghosts you. On these occasions, you are going to feel like a fool. Instead of getting all caught up in the belief that your entire self has been destroyed and the mortification of the experience is so horrific you will never be able to face anyone ever again, how about just accepting the fact that sometimes we all look like a bit of a fool?

Despite how wounded your ego might feel, it is possible to laugh at your own mistakes and failings. *Yeah... that was a total flop. I really stuffed that up. Wow! I did not anticipate that at all...* It is possible not to take yourself so seriously.

The more fool-hardy you become, the greater your courage grows.

You
cannot fail

What if you knew with absolute certainty that you could not fail?

That if only you kept going, you would succeed?

What if you knew that failure is part of it, the growing, the becoming, and that mistakes are just lessons teaching you what you need to learn?

Why not, instead of convincing yourself you can't, ask *if it can happen for others, why not me?*

What if you decided to give yourself the gift, of believing in yourself, of turning up, and showing up, for the dreams you have made?

Your goals may be lofty but they are possible.

If you haven't given up, if you are still on the journey, you haven't failed at all, you simply haven't got there... yet.

Keep going

The trick is to keep on going. Any fool can begin a thing. But the profound changes many of us seek – new careers, new skills, new relationships, new adventures, new outlooks – only happen through continual and repeated effort.

Each time you pick yourself up and keep keep going, you teach your fear that while you can't stop it talking, it doesn't mean you have to listen. Eventually fear's voice grows quieter.

You may even notice a new voice inside your head filled with thoughts of how grateful you are that you get to do the thing you are doing. Not that you *HAVE* to, though it may have started out that way, but that you *GET* to do this thing. You *get* to decide. You *get* to choose.

You go to sleep feeling content with all you have done, knowing that tomorrow you will wake up and your fear will be there to greet you again. You know you can face it. And each time you do, your capacity to do so grows.

You are complicated

Much as you may long for simplicity, true growth comes from embracing complexity.

You are complicated.
Life is complicated.

Become aware that in each moment, you contain a myriad of thoughts, feelings and responses, many of which are contradictory, all of which hold truth.

You can simultaneously feel afraid, hopeful, determined, happy, uncertain and angry. You can feel wounded by life, uncertain of what the future holds, aware that you are living in an unjust world, but still grateful for all that you have.

An awareness that you contain multitudes gives you a way to shake fear's grip on you, or more importantly, your grip on fear. Expand into the awareness that you are not one thing.

Hold fear in one hand while you reach for other parts of yourself.

Find the balance that will allow you to keep moving forward.

Accept reality

Most things worth doing in life are harder than we would like, take longer than we would hope, and require a constantly humbling process of coming up short and finding the fortitude and resilience to keep going. It is a bitter pill to swallow, but there you have it. Reality is like that.

Instead of giving up when obstacles arise, accept them as inevitable and keep moving forward. When it comes to growth and change, you must be the tortoise, not the hare. The runner of marathons not of sprints.

The end result is worth it.
You are worth it.

It is okay
to rest

Despite what fear tells you, it's okay to rest. To have days when you are phoning it in. To have times when you feel defeated. To kick your couch in frustration, wailing *It shouldn't be this hard!*

Feel it.
Wallow in it.
Let yourself nap.

I am not going to lie, I am not great at this. Recently I got sick. Though my body ached and my throat screamed, I felt guilty not working so I brought my laptop to bed, making martyred, half-hearted attempts at putting words on a page until my partner grabbed the computer from me and ordered me to rest.

The next day I sat in the garden, warming my face in a patch of sunlight breaking through the winter grey. Bees landed on fragrant daphne. My dog brought me a stick. The world kept rotating, without me needing to turn the crank.

When you feel a lack of momentum, your health is suffering or your spirits are low, don't buy into fear's stories. Constant vigilance is not required. Lack of motivation or low energy is not a sign you are meant to give up or that you are a worthless, no-good failure. This is part of the journey.

No mountain is climbed a single day. Climb, then rest. Climb, then rest.

It is okay to take a break. To give your body time to process. To reconcile the person you once were with the person you are becoming.

Celebrate the view you can see from the place you are now. Reflect on the lessons you have learned. The skills you have gained. How inured you have come to the pain of the climb. Look back for a moment at how far you have come.

Think on the words of Brianna Wiest who said, "One day, the mountain that is in front of you will be so far behind you, it will barely be visible in the distance. But the person you become in learning to get over it? That will stay with you forever. And that is the point of the mountain."

PART 3

Courage
in Action

*Scared is what you're
feeling. Brave is what
you're doing.*

—

Emma Donoghue

courage

/ˈkʌrɪdʒ/

noun

1. the ability to **do something** that frightens you

2. mental or moral strength to **venture, persevere, and withstand** danger, fear, or difficulty.

3. the choice and willingness to **confront** pain, uncertainty or intimidation

4. mental or moral strength to **resist** opposition, or hardship

There are many definitions of courage, but the one thing they have in common is that they involve **action.**

You are already brave

When I was thirteen, I ran to my neighbour's house in the small hours of the morning, asking her to call the police on my father, who had broken into our house to hurt my mum. When people think of courage this is often the kind of thing they think of – a daring, high stakes dash in the middle of the night.

The courage of everyday life is less heat-of-the-moment and more deliberate and conscious choice. Commonplace courage is a decision to risk putting your heart, not just your body, on the line.

When I finished a science degree and pursued my dream of becoming an actor instead, that took courage.

When I started speaking my truth, sharing my stories, allowing my vulnerability to be seen (and judged and misunderstood) by others, that took courage.

When I told a friend I was no longer willing to put up with the way she spoke to me, and if she didn't change, we could no longer have a relationship, that took courage.

When I married someone I loved, despite feeling terrified of being abandoned, that took courage.

When I had kids, knowing that I wanted more than anything to be a good parent, yet feeling deeply afraid I might stuff it up because I didn't have good parenting role models of my own, that took courage.

You have these moments too. Dozens of them. Think on them now.

The conversations. The creations. The adventures. The decisions.

All these scary brave things you have done. The deep yelping war cries it took to psych yourself into believing you were capable, it was possible, that the good things you wanted could happen for someone like you.

From the outside, your bravest moments might look easy. Only you know how much fear you had to overcome.

Often our most courageous acts are invisible to anyone but ourselves.

Courage is living life in alignment with your heart

Courage is taking up residence inside your own heart, listening to the wisdom you find there, honouring the truth you know from that place, and acting on the inspirations and urges of your most deeply felt knowing.

Courage is a decision to take risks that in your bones feels right, even though they terrify the crap out of you.

Courage is choosing to share your heart and mind with others, with no guarantees of how they will respond.

The reward you receive for daring to reveal yourself in this way is a truthful, authentic and aligned life.

Let today be the day
you come back
inside your own skin.

Let today be the day
you start living
from your own heart.

JOURNAL PROMPT

Settle into your heart and ask:

- What lights me up?
- What brings me joy?
- What truly matters to me?
- What gifts do I want to share with the world?
- What do I want to change?
- What truth have I been denying?
- What wisdom do I need to hear?
- What courageous way will I reveal my heart today?

Acceptance
as courage

Growing up, I longed to feel in control. I wanted to control people and situations and as much of the world as possible. Control meant certainty. Certainty felt safe.

There is comfort of sorts in believing life is entirely in our control. But not only is this idea a delusion, it is also a recipe for unending stress and anxiety. So much energy is wasted trying to alter aspects of life we don't have the power to change.

You can be a safe driver... you can still end up getting side-swiped by a car.

You can support your partner through an illness... you can't guarantee they get better.

You can be brave enough to be vulnerable and tell someone you like them... you can't force them to like you back.

You can set a new boundary in a relationship... you can't control whether a person will respect or violate it.

My mum went to Alcoholics Anonymous for a while when I was growing up. One night she brought home a poem from one of the meetings she attended.

Grant me the serenity to
accept the things I cannot change

Courage to change the things I can

And the wisdom to know the difference

The courage of acceptance asks that you become crystal clear on what you can and can't control. Instead of wasting energy thinking about how people *should* be or how things *should* have gone, acceptance builds upon reality of *what is,* including the limitations of the power you have over the world.

Acceptance involves making a conscious choice to willingly and repeatedly let go of those parts of the life equation you can do nothing about, and to narrow your focus only on the aspects you can impact.

Acceptance isn't easy. It often feels like grief. Acceptance asks you to give in to what is. But it doesn't mean giving up.

The more closely you focus only on those things in your control and let go of the rest, the more power and energy you will find you have.

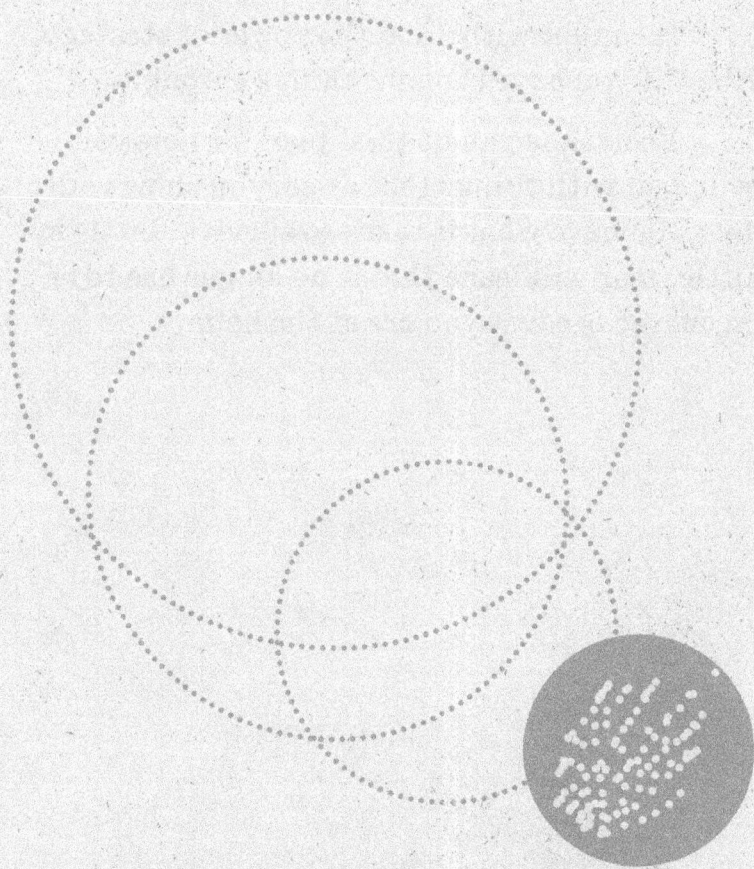

Courage begins with a plan

Fear doesn't really want to stop you. It doesn't want to control you. It wants to know you are in charge and you have a plan.

Fear does not stand up to scrutiny.

It cannot withstand the power of strategy. Show it you have thought things through.

Each time you do this, plan for how you will deal with things that arise, you show your fear you have what it takes to survive. Little by little, fear will learn that it no longer has to be in charge because you are at the helm.

Claim the ground you want to change

There is no point in wasting energy on courageous action until you are clear on what you want. As you engage with this process, continually ask yourself if the things you say you want are truly important to you or if you have simply become conditioned to the idea you *should* want them based on other people's ideas and expectations. The more brutally honest you can be with yourself, the more powerful this process becomes.

JOURNAL PROMPT

Take out a piece of paper and write under the following headings. Health. Career. Home. Finance. Relationships with others. Relationship with yourself. Attitude to life.

Think of stuck points you want to shift and goals you want to achieve. Get specific and break big goals into achievable micro-actions e.g. "Want a better job" might include questions like: What don't I like about my old job? What would my ideal job/ workplace look like? Who do I know who might be able to give me some advice?

Create a to-do list from the answers to your questions

- Contact Klaudia

- Contact Sarah

- Research good CVs

- Update CV

- Look on job seeking sites.

Take one action right now.
Then another. Then another.
If something doesn't work,
try something else.

Do this over and over.
This is how change happens.
This is how courage grows.
Small repeated actions.
One step at a time.

If you want to deep dive into a more intensive process on this you can download your free courageous planning template at **ruthclare.com/ resources**

The well
of courage

Each of us has a well of courage. No matter how much you have endured, how afraid your experiences have made you, this well of courage is deeper. It is untouched by anything your parents did to you, or society, or those arseholes at school who shouldered you in the hallway and wrote mean stuff about you on the blackboard.

Each time you did not let fear defeat you, each time you struggled and overcame, each time you faced another day, then another, you unknowingly drew from this well. When you use the words *dig deep* it is of this well you speak.

This well is not fixed in size. The more you use it, the deeper it goes.

**The more you practice courage,
the more courage you will find you have.**

3 steps
of courage
in action

1.   RECOGNIZE your fear

---

2.   Remind yourself you are
BIGGER THAN your fear

---

3.   Take an action to
COUNTER your fear

SCENARIO 1:

1. I fear being rejected.
2. I tell myself rejection is not the end of the world and I will survive.
3. I make a call / post a video / send an email / pitch a story

1... 2... 3

SCENARIO 2:

1. I fear saying the wrong thing.
2. I remind myself nobody is perfect and what is right to one person will be wrong to another so I may as well just say what I think.
3. I share my thoughts / write my ideas / don't read reviews on things I have written.

1... 2... 3

SCENARIO 3:

1. I fear quitting my job.
2. I reassure myself I don't have to make any rash decisions but I can stay open to the possibility of change being good.
3. I get clear on what I would like to do instead / learn new skills / work on my CV / tell people I am looking for another job.

1... 2... 3

Develop
a tolerance
for discomfort

We would all love endless easy days filled with rainbows and sunshine, but life is not instagram. In the world of humans, there is struggle and strife.

If there is one skill that will build your courage the fastest, it is becoming comfortable being uncomfortable.

Theodore Roosevelt said, "It is only through labour and painful effort, by grim energy and resolute courage, that we move on to better things."

Painful. Grim. Resolute. Doesn't sound like very much fun.

Yeah, well. Neither is the alternative. Fearful. Helpless. Trapped.

There is no skill more overlooked or

undervalued than building a capacity to tolerate misery, shut up and keep going. This doesn't mean staying stuck in situations you hate. This means tolerating the misery of how afraid you feel, acknowledging how much you hate where you are, deciding you aren't going to put up with things then taking action, even though you feel uncomfortable the whole time. This process is gruelling, but necessary.

Changing, growing, learning, doing what needs to be done to achieve grand visions, is never a straight line and it always involves effort. You must steel yourself against hardship and frustration, worry and doubt, and realise that each time you pick yourself up and keep going, you are taking another step toward the life you want.

Be your weird and wonderful self

Brené Brown says, "Courage starts with showing up and letting ourselves be seen." Being seen isn't just about being visible. It is about revealing and expressing your *true* self with others, not the clever, stylish, polished, fake-Frankenstein monster self you have created to impress.

In the whole of time there will never be another person who has your personality, your experiences, your quirks and fascinations, your impulses and dreams. Don't keep trying to hide that. The world needs your unique perspective. To have more joy in your life, you must be brave enough to own those things that make you happy and to do more of them.

Stop trying to live other people's lives and step fully into your own.

Becoming
Courageous You

Scientific imaging has shown our brains struggle to identify the difference between imagination and real life. This is why athletes, musicians and performers visualise their performance over and over in their minds. The same neuronal pathways created during physical practice are strengthened through picturing themselves performing those tasks in their mind's eye.

You can use the process of daily rehearsal to build the courageous person you are becoming.

VISUALISATION EXERCISE

Close your eyes and picture the most courageous version of yourself.

- What are you wearing?
- What does the space you inhabit look like?
- How do you speak?
- How do you feel in your body?
- How do you move?

- What does *Courageous You* wish you knew about your own strengths?

- How would *Courageous You* respond to the biggest challenge you are currently facing?

- What would *Courageous You* do with this day to help make your dreams come true?

- How would *Courageous You* act to counter your fear?

Picture it.

Visualise it.

Become it.

Do what you rehearse in your mind in real life.

You have become *Courageous You.*

Set things in motion

Newton's first law of motion states that a body at rest remains at rest whereas a body in motion remains in motion. This is true in life not just in the laboratory.

A body in motion stays in motion. Committing to action builds momentum.

Momentum builds the energy you need to solve the problems you encounter along the way.

Once you are in action, all sorts of wonderful things begin to stir. You will be at a cafe chatting to a guy standing beside you in line. He will ask what you are doing. You will tell him you are writing a book. He will respond by saying he is a writer too and did you want to join his writing group.

You will begin looking for a new job. You will tell your friend about your search. They will know a guy who knows a guy and suddenly... voila!

You will start your own business. You will encounter blocks to success. You will stumble upon books or conversations or events or situations or opportunities or people that can help you keep moving forward.

This magic only happens once we set things in motion.

Life is ultimately measured by our actions. Not our intentions. Not the things we thought about doing, wanted to do, but didn't actually do.

Don't leave the bow in the arrow. Fire it. Commit to your dreams and goals. Show up for them. Clumsily and imperfectly, but at least present and willing. Decide today that the reward is worth the risk and there are worse things than looking foolish. Things like a life half-lived, a world of regret and a lifetime of longing for what might have been.

Courageous action only takes ten seconds

The first part of the action— convincing yourself to pick up the phone, saying no for the first time, putting your hand up for the project— that is the part that requires courage. After that, you are in the process of doing, and everything is easier once the game is in play.

Your fear has an unending number of disaster stories to tell you about why you shouldn't do something. The longer you listen to those stories, the more courage it will take to act.

Limit the amount of time you are willing to indulge your fear. Then cut across your fear thoughts and act.

Yes, Yes. I hear what you are saying. You think I will make the phone call and the person will scream at me and tell me I am a fool and slam the phone down on me. You might be right, but I am going to do it anyway.' *Makes phone call.

Ten seconds is long enough.

Don't give your
fear the floor
too long.

10 seconds...
GO.

Transforming fear into excitement

When you begin acting with courage, fear will go into overdrive. Do not be surprised by this.

Stay curious. Fear and excitement evoke similar sensations in our body. Could the sensations you are calling fear also be excitement at your own daring?

Don't believe your fear is excitement? Trick yourself into believing it. Our bodies aren't very good at telling the difference between pretend and authentic movements. In her TEDx talk on power posing, social psychologist, Amy Cuddy, found that simply putting your limbs in the position of a powerful person tricks your emotions into feeing more powerful.

This echoes a technique I learned during my acting days called "cooking yourself up". "Cooking yourself up" involves drawing on memories when you had similar feelings to the emotions of the character you are playing, physicalising the body postures of that emotion until you feel a genuine resonance in your body.

This same strategy works to reframe fear as excitement.

PHYSICAL EXERCISE TO
TURN FEAR INTO EXCITEMENT

Even if your knees are knocking in terror, put your hands in the air like you just don't care and dance around. Put on some music if you want. Breathe into your belly, whack a pen between your teeth forcing your muscles into smile position. Let out a little woohoo if the impulse strikes you! Say aloud, *I am so excited.* (Perhaps remove the pen first or you may end up dribbling).

You may feel silly. You may end up laughing at yourself. Good!

Laughter shows your body that there is no danger. Laughter helps convince your biology that you are not afraid. Keep doing this process for a few minutes, until your emotion shifts.

**Not paranoia...
possibility.**

**Not fear...
excitement.**

Confidence comes after the fact

You may have been waiting to feel more confident before you change your relationships, achieve great things or create beautiful art. Confidence is not something bestowed upon you at the beginning of a journey. It is a reward you receive while you are on the path.

Believing you can do something often doesn't happen until after you have already done it. I hoped I could write a book. I was willing to try writing a book. But I didn't *know* I could write a book until after I wrote one.

Actions that stretch you and grow you are usually taken while you are wracked with self-doubt, worry and fear. You don't feel confident and then do them. You do them and then feel confident.

Be
Thomas

Is the change you want to achieve possible? In the end you will only ever answer the question through action.

Not one half-hearted attempt. Sweat-inducing, fear-evoking action taken over and over again. Without the capacity to do this, Thomas Edison may not have picked himself up off the floor that 999th time so he might go on to invent the lightbulb. Yes, 999 times he tried. 999 times he failed. But he didn't give up.

He learned from each of his mistakes and adjusted his approach. And now we flick a switch and have light.

Light is good. Your idea is probably good too. Don't give up on it. Don't give up on yourself.

Be Thomas.

Courage questions

- How does this action align with the bigger picture I want for my life?

- What rewards can come from taking this risk?

- What will taking this action prove to myself?

- What joy can be found if I go on this journey?

- Will this action teach me something, even if it doesn't go the way I want?

- How might I regret not taking this action three years from now?

- If the worst-case scenario did happen because I took this action, what are five practical things I could do to handle that?

Action speaks louder than fear

As a kid the rule in our house was we had to eat everything on our plate. Didn't like it? Too bad. Put it in your mouth and chew.

Taking action while feeling fear is kind of like that. Not always enjoyable, but possible.

It helps to remember that you aren't the only one being forced to eat what's on your plate. There are people all around you enduring the misery of committing to brave action while their teeth are chattering in terror. There they are, turning up to chemotherapy, going for their driver's licence, separating from their partner, performing their first flamenco dance.

Do you think these people are waltzing into these situations without any fear? No. They too are taking courageous steps with leaden legs, after sleepless nights.

Despite this, they keep going. Shovelling their fear from forks to mouth. Chewing through action until they finally hit the mark.

Some of the most extraordinary people in the world have faced the biggest obstacles imaginable. They were able to do all the things they did because they faced each day with a tiny bit more courage than fear. That is all.

You are not alone my friend. It's a journey we must all take. At least knowing this is something. Now do it.

Take action.
Do it now.

Action steps

While there are some parts of life you don't have the power to change, there are many, many areas of life you can impact in major ways. Right now.

JOURNAL PROMPT

Think of the place you feel most stuck or unhappy. Take out a pen and paper and write...

- Ten things you might do differently in this moment.

- Ten fresh ways you to see your situation.

- Ten small actions you could take today.

- Ten things you have already achieved.

- Ten benefits of trying something different.

- Ten things you could do if your worst fears came true.

There are always possibilities, plan B's and ways forward. Don't let not knowing if the path you are taking is right be the excuse that stops you.

Take action,
reflect.

Take action,
adjust.

Take action,
create the life you want.

Taming
the beast

You wake with a gnawing feeling in your gut. Fear begins its work, filling your mind with mistakes you might make and ways it can all go wrong. Let the rush happen.

Treat your fear like an untamed animal. Be aware, without engaging with it. Know the most effective way to put fear in its place. To tame the beast, you must commit to taking actions that set your heart racing. Consciously and deliberately choose to face risk, uncertainty and vulnerability.

Do the things that scare and grow you at the same time.

Show fear you choose courage. Ground yourself in the present moment. Move away from the relentlessness of your thoughts and return to your body and the anchoring resource of your breath. Remind yourself that you are safe, your fear isn't a fact and being brave does not equal death.

Know that you are enough and that no matter what, it will all turn out okay. Because despite fear's misgivings, you are more powerful than you think and more capable than you know.

You got this.

**When your fear tells you to run,
face the hard and scary things.**

**When your fear tells you to hide,
do the hard and scary things.**

**This is the way you tame the beast
and grow your courage each day.**

Courage
in action

When we heed the call of courage, *feel the fear and do it anyway,* we learn that the possibilities for our life are endless. Possibilities, however, are only pipe dreams unless we realise them through action.

EXAMPLES OF
COURAGE IN ACTION

**Write down your dreams and
turn them into plans**

- Join a group of people who have the same goals as you

- Learn new skills and use them

- Share your truth, your creations, your beautiful self with the world

- Ask for what you want

- Set boundaries

- Try something new

- Find a therapist, mentor or friend who has your back

- Figure things out as you go

- Ask for help if you need it

- Do things that make you happy

- Remind yourself of your own awesomeness

To build you courage muscles, feel fear, take action. That is all. When used regularly these muscles have the power to move mountains, amass fortunes and change lives.

What small acts of courage will you take today?

What fear will you face?

What life will you create?

May you...

dream impossible dreams
and make them a reality

make friends with fear,
uncertainty and change

experience the homecoming
of returning to your body

find joy in small daily wonders

do things each day that scare you

feel safe to be who you really are

share yourself with the world

celebrate your expansion

shine bright

**Let your dreams guide you,
your gut inform you
and your heart
lead the way.**

My wish
for you

Courage is the doorway to your
destiny. Do not shrink from it
because it asks too much of you.
Walk willingly toward the tests you
face. Stay the course when the odds
seem stacked against you.

* * *

Know that you will never be
completely ready. There will never be
a perfect time. Do it anyway.

* * *

Put your arrow in the bow and fire
it. When you fail to hit your target,
shrug it off. Learning to take
life less seriously is the strongest
antidote to fear.

* * *

* * *

Remember that nothing is
permanent, change is constant and
there is always a chance to make
things better. All you have to do is
keep getting up and starting over.

* * *

Learn to love the process of
becoming who you are. Celebrate
your small-but-great victories.
Champion your own growth.

* * *

* * *

Return to the wildly beating place
inside yourself. Come to know your
own heart. Notice how the cracks
and fissures of this landscape, scars
of heartbreak survived, are the very
places where your light now shines
the brightest.

* * *

Own what you really want from life
and go after it. Know that each time
you pick yourself up after a failure is
a success. Remind yourself that the
person you are becoming as you dare
to pursue your dreams, is the whole
point of dreams in the first place.

Stop comparing yourself to others
and finding yourself lacking. Focus
only on where you started to where
you are now. Take time to marvel at
how much you have grown.

• • •

Do not listen to advice or follow
in the footsteps of people who
are trapped and shrunken, living
beneath the thumb of their own fear.
Be brave enough to forge your own
path and light your own way. Find
others who have been where you
want to go and build a community
around you.

• • •

If you are lucky, you will have four
thousand weeks of life on earth.
This is both long and short. Don't
fall into the trap of overestimating
what you can achieve in a year and
underestimating what you can
achieve in a decade. Remind yourself
that big dreams and major changes
take time. Don't give up. We need
what you have to offer.

There has never been another
person in all of history who has had
your exact genetics, experiences or
perspective. You have wisdom and
ideas the world needs to know. Don't
let your dreams, your voice or your
passions die inside you. Share them
with the world. Let us all benefit
from your gifts.

* * *

No matter the challenges you have
faced, know that no one has the
power to stop you from creating
a joyful and fulfilling life except
yourself. Your life doesn't happen by
chance, it happens by choice.
Make a choice now.

* * *

Turn your fear
into courage.

Make your dreams
a reality.

Become the person
you were always
meant to be.

Acknowledgements

To my co-creator in life and art, the amazing graphic designer and illustrator responsible for the visual beauty of this book, my wonderful husband Matt Clare. I am in awe of your incredible talent and unendingly grateful for your attention to detail (and patience for all the drafts I made you do). Thank you for your support and faith in me. Your love helps me be brave.

Thanks Magdalena McGuire, beautiful writer and dear friend, who read early drafts and helped me believe this book was worth sharing.

Much gratitude to Sarah Coffey, for her feedback on the manuscript, and for being part of my creativity and life support team, alongside Klaudia Furness, who always tells me my crazy ideas are possible.

Beck Jobson, three cheers for listening to me drone on endlessly about my ten thousand ideas while occasionally breaking into song, and for your formatting advice.

Biggest respect and gratitude to ANVAM, for many years of support, for both my writing and speaking work, and my mission to make things better for veterans and veteran families.

Also, thanks to my writing group, Bianca Denny, Elisabeth Hanscombe, Gay Lynch, Matthew Roberts and David Sornig for your wisdom and passion for ideas and writing.

There are many other people I am sure I have forgotten. If that is you, please forgive me and know the oversight is the result of a shoddy memory rather than an uncaring heart. I love you, and everyone, and the whole world really. Let us now all sit together and sing Kumbaya.

What did you think of *Turn Fear into Courage*?

If you enjoyed this book, I would be very grateful if you could leave a short review on Amazon or Goodreads, or wherever else you review things. I would especially love to know if it motivated you to do something courageous in your own life because I am unendingly inspired by all the cool, brave stuff people do. Thank you so much for your support!

Let's stay in touch

I would love to stay connected. Sign up to my free newsletter and find out more about me at **ruthclare.com** or connect with me on the socials **@ruthclareauthor**

Also by RUTH CLARE

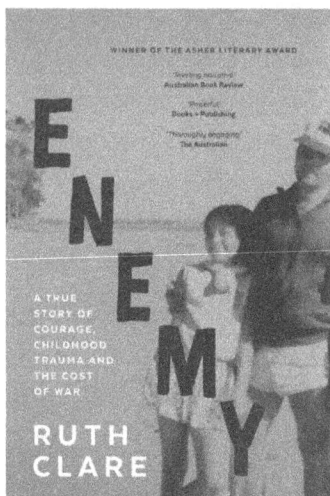

ENEMY

WINNER OF THE ASHER LITERARY AWARD

A TRUE STORY OF COURAGE, CHILDHOOD TRAUMA AND THE COST OF WAR

RUTH CLARE

BEYOND FIGHT FLIGHT FREEZE FAWN

How to regulate your nervous system and reclaim your life

RUTH CLARE

Ruth's award-winning memoir about growing up as the child of a traumatized veteran and the unrecognised price families of veterans can pay when the war comes home.

Available worldwide as a book and audiobook.

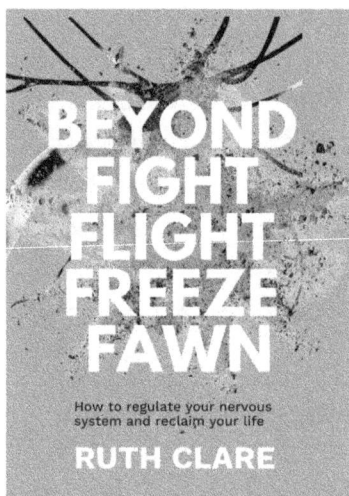

A neuroscience-based guide to trauma recovery including practical somatic and mindfulness exercises to regulate your emotions and shift your nervous system out of survival mode so you can live with more calm and joy.

Available via ruthclare.com